What Are Literature Pockets?

In *Literature Pockets—Nonfiction* you will find activities for 11 categories of books and for "Finding Information in the Library." The finished activities are stored in a labeled pocket made from construction paper. (See directions below.) Add the charming cover and fasten the pockets together. Your students now have their own Nonfiction book to treasure.

How to Make the Pockets

1. Use a 12″ x 18″ (30.5 x 45.5 cm) piece of construction paper for each pocket. Fold up 6″ (15 cm) to make a 12″ (30.5 cm) square.

2. Staple the right side of the pocket closed.

3. Punch two or three holes in the left side of the pocket.

4. Glue the title strip onto the pocket. The title strip is found on the bookmark page for each book.

5. Store each completed project in the pocket for that book.

How to Make the Cover

1. Reproduce the cover decoration on page 3 for each student.

2. Students color and cut out the cover and glue it to a 12″ (30.5 cm) square piece of construction paper.

3. Punch two or three holes in the left side of the cover.

4. When all the pockets are completed, fasten the cover and the pockets together. You might use string, ribbon, twine, raffia, or metal rings.

Basic Steps for Each Book

This book presents activities for various types of nonfiction as they are organized according to the Dewey decimal system. Follow these basic steps with each category.

- Show several different types of books found in the section of the library being studied. Summarize the books briefly and ask students to identify any similarities that would account for the books being categorized together.

- Make the category bookmark. Have students cut out the bookmark and glue it to a 5" x 11½" (13 x 29.5 cm) piece of construction paper. Review the description of the category and the list of books. Send students off to the library to see how many of the books on the bookmark can be found in your library. They may add other titles they find to the blank lines on the bookmark.

- Ask students to read at least two different types of books from each category you study.

- Complete the writing activities and art experiences provided for each pocket.

Finding Information
in the library

People

Religion and Myths

Folklore

Language

Nature and Animals

Mathematics

Science and Technology

Arts, Sports, and
Recreation

Poetry and Plays

History and Travel

Biography

Reading

Myths

History   Science

Animals   Poetry

Mathematics

Language

Biography

Nonfiction

Name _____

Finding Information in the Library

Bookmark .... **page 5**
Make the bookmark following the instructions on page 2. Review the reading list provided on the bookmark. Ask students to read one book about the library.

Dewey Decimal System—
A Folded Book .... **page 6**
Make two folds to complete this tiny book about Melvil Dewey and the Dewey decimal system. Read and discuss the contents as a class.

Dewey Decimal Search .... **pages 7 and 8**
Each group of students is assigned one section of the Dewey decimal system to explore. Compile group observations to create a class chart of the types of books found in each section. Students make their own copy to place in their pocket book.

Finding Information
in the Library .... **pages 9 and 10**
Students practice using the card catalog or automated search system to locate books on a self-selected topic.

Parts of a Nonfiction Book ...**pages 11 and 12**
What's in a nonfiction book? What kinds of information can be found? This activity helps students answer both of these questions.

In the Library

Explore books about libraries and what they contain. The 000s also include general books of information of different kinds. Go exploring to see what you can learn.

- *Check It Out—The Book about Libraries* by Gail Gibbons
- *The Inside-Outside Book of Libraries* by Julie Cummins and Roxi Munro
- *Libraries* by Lucia Raatma
- *Libraries Take Us Far* by Lee Sullivan Hill
- *Library: From Ancient Scrolls to the World Wide Web* by John Malam
- *The New York Public Library Kid's Guide to Research* by Deborah Heiligman
- *Scholastic Treasury of Quotations for Children* compiled by Adrienne Betz
- *The Top 10 of Everything 2001* by Russell Ash

_____

_____

_____

_____

Finding Information In the Library

Melvil Dewey and the Dewey Decimal System

000 General
100 Philosophy and Psychology
200 Religion and Mythology
300 Social Science
400 Language
500 Natural Science and Mathematics
600 Science and Technology
700 Arts, Sports, and Recreation
800 Literature
900 Geography and History

fold

fold

Melvil Dewey

Melvil Dewey was born in New York on December 10, 1851. He died on December 26, 1931. He was a librarian who invented a classification system for library books that is still used today.

Mr. Dewey helped establish the American Library Association. He co-founded and edited *Library Journal.* In 1887 he founded the first library school at Columbia College (now called Columbia University).

Dewey Decimal System

The Dewey decimal classification system is used to organize books in libraries. It is used in many countries around the world. The system is divided into ten classes. Each class is then divided into smaller divisions using decimal points.

The Dewey decimal number assigned to a book is known as its **call number.**

600 Science and Technology

630 Agriculture

636 Animal Husbandry

636.7 Dogs

Dewey Decimal Search

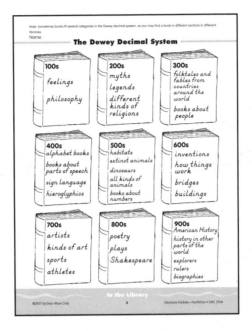

Students explore different divisions of the Dewey decimal system. Compile the information they find on a class chart. Students then make a copy of the final chart to place in this pocket.

Materials
- chart paper
- page 8, reproduced for each student
- black marking pen
- writing paper and pencils

Steps to Follow
1. Using a black marking pen and chart paper, create a chart with a box for each section of the Dewey decimal system from the 100s to the 900s. (See page 8.)

2. Ask students to recall what they have learned about the Dewey decimal system (books have numbers; we use the Dewey decimal system to find a book in the library; it classifies books into categories). Direct their attention to the chart. Explain that they will be going to the library to discover what types of books are found in each section of numbers.

3. Divide students into small groups. Assign each group one section to explore. Their task is to examine the books in their section and list the characteristics of the books shelved there.

4. Compile the results of each group's research on the chart. Students transfer the information to their own charts using the form on page 8.

Name:

The Dewey Decimal System

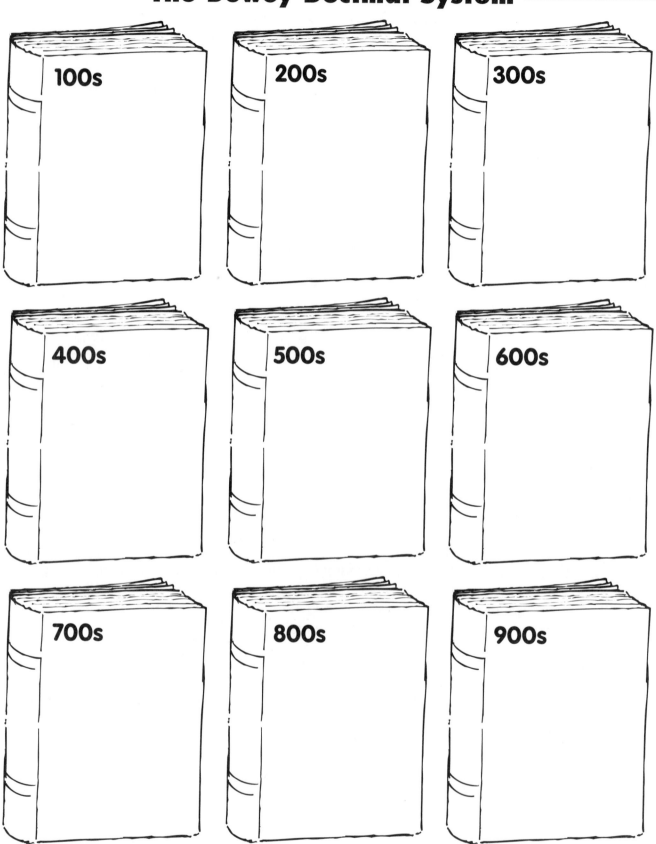

Finding Information in the Library

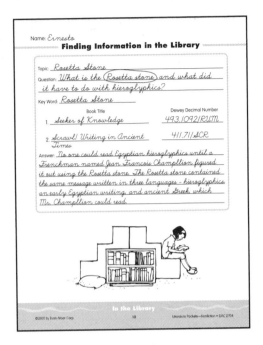

Students practice using the card catalog or automated search system in the library to find information about a specific topic.

Materials

- page 10, reproduced for each student
- pencil

Steps to Follow

1. Model how to use the card catalog or automated search system in your library.

2. Using the form on page 10, students select a topic and write a question they would like answered about that topic. After writing the topic and question on their record sheets, students circle the key word in the question. This is the word they will use to begin their search in the library.

3. Using the card catalog or automated search system in the library, students use the key word to find books on their topic. They are to select two books they think will answer their question. They record the titles and Dewey decimal numbers on their record forms.

4. Finally, students are to skim the books to find the answer to their question. If they are successful, they are to write the answer on the record form. If they are unable to find the answer in these two books, they are to select two more books, continuing until they have been successful. Additional titles and Dewey decimal numbers may be written on the back of their record forms.

Literature Pockets—Nonfiction • EMC 2704

Name: _____

Finding Information in the Library

Topic: _____

Question: _____

_____

Key Word: _____

Book Title	Dewey Decimal Number
1. _____	_____
2. _____	_____

Answer: _____

_____

_____

_____

_____

_____

_____

     Literature Pockets—Nonfiction • EMC 2704

Parts of a Nonfiction Book

Students complete the form on page 12 to show they understand what the various parts of a nonfiction book contain.

Materials

- a nonfiction book used by everyone in class (science or social studies)
- page 12, reproduced for each student
- an assortment of nonfiction books from the library
- pencils

Steps to Follow

1. Using a book such as a science or social studies text, have students create a list of the different parts of the book (text, captions, index, etc.). Write these on the chalkboard. Challenge students to find information in each of the parts. Record examples of the information on the board.

2. Working with a partner, students select a nonfiction book from the library and complete the form on page 12. (Both partners complete the form so each has a copy for the pocket book.) They are to circle a different book part in each box and write one piece of information they found in that location. Have extra copies of page 12 available for students who want to complete the entire list of possible information sources within a book.

text
picture
captions

In the Library

Name: _____

Information from Nonfiction Books

_____ Title	_____ Dewey #
Where in the book did you find the information? Circle the source.	**What did you learn?** Write one fact.
text　　　　　　　pictures captions　　　　　headings glossary　　　　　cover index　　　　　　title page table of contents	
text　　　　　　　pictures captions　　　　　headings glossary　　　　　cover index　　　　　　title page table of contents	
text　　　　　　　pictures captions　　　　　headings glossary　　　　　cover index　　　　　　title page table of contents	
text　　　　　　　pictures captions　　　　　headings glossary　　　　　cover index　　　　　　title page table of contents	
text　　　　　　　pictures captions　　　　　headings glossary　　　　　cover index　　　　　　title page table of contents	

In the Library

People

Bookmark .... page 14
Make the bookmark following the instructions on page 2. Review the reading list provided on the bookmark. Ask students to read two nonfiction books about people.

Catalog Cards.....................pages 15 and 16
Students create "catalog cards" as one way to summarize books read in this category. You will use the same form for each nonfiction pocket.

A Real-Life Hero? .... pages 17–19
Who is a hero? What makes a hero? In this activity, students explore both of those questions.

Survey of Opinions .... page 20
Many books in this category express how people feel about an issue. Work together to select a topic of interest to the students. Students conduct interviews to determine how others feel about the issue, and then write about what they learned.

People

What do we think about ourselves? What do we think about other people? Check the 100s and 300s to find some answers to these questions.

- *Children of the Wild West* by Russell Freedman

- *Dear Mrs. Parks: A Dialogue with Today's Youth* by Rosa Parks

- *How It Feels to Be Adopted* by Jill Krementz

- *In the Next Three Seconds* by Rowland Morgan

- *I Was Dreaming to Come to America: Memories from Ellis Island* selected by Veronica Lawlor

- *Kids at Work: Lewis Hine and the Crusade Against Child Labor* by Russell Freedman

- *Let It Shine: Stories of Black Women Freedom Fighters* by Andrea Davis Pinkney

- *They Shall Be Heard: Susan B. Anthony & Elizabeth Cady Stanton* by Kate Connell

- *Voices from the Fields: Children of Migrant Farmworkers Tell Their Stories* by S. Beth Atkin

- *A Young Person's Guide to Philosophy* edited by Jeremy Weate

_____

_____

_____

_____

People

Catalog Cards

Catalog Card

Author: _Pinkney, Jer_

Title: _Aesop's Fabl_

Imprint (published): _Sea St_
_c 2_

Description: _87 pages;_
illustrat

Subject: _Fables; Folk_

Notes: _Nearly 60 fable_
Aesop retold by M

Call Number | _398.24_

Your name: _Geo_

Catalog Car

Author: _Parks, Rosa_

Title: _Dear Mrs. Park_

Imprint (published): _Lee & L_
_c 1_

Description: _111 page_
illustratio

Subject: _Rosa Parks; Civil_

Notes: _Shares letters bet_
Parks and children in whi
questions and offers encou

Call Number | _323.09_

Your name: _Tam_

Catalog Card

Author: _Gibbons, Gail_

Title: _Check It Out!: The_
Book about Libraries

Imprint (published): _Harcourt Brace Jovanovich_
_c 1985_

Description: _32 pages; color_
illustrations

Subject: _Libraries_

Notes: _This book describes_
what is in libraries

Call Number | _027 / GIB_

Your name: _Anna B._

Begin a class nonfiction card catalog as students read and review books from each section of the library. A copy of the form will be completed and placed in each of the topic pockets.

Materials

- transparency of page 16
- page 16, reproduced for each student (keep extra copies for students reading more than one book in the category)
- pencil

Steps to Follow

1. Prepare a storage container (a file box or notebook) or a database for copies of the completed cards. Include dividers to separate the different types of books people read (people, religion and myths, etc.). File the cards in alphabetical order.

2. Make an overhead transparency of the form on page 16 to use as a model. Select a book about a person. If the book is short, read it to the class. If not, give a summary of the contents. Using the book as an example, complete the "catalog card."

3. Place a supply of card forms in an accessible spot. Students complete a card for a nonfiction book they read about people. Make a copy of each card to keep in a class file. Students put the original card in their People pockets.

People

Catalog Card

Author: _____

Title: _____

Imprint (published): _____

Description: _____

Subject: _____

Notes: _____

Call Number

Your name: _____

Catalog Card

Author: _____

Title: _____

Imprint (published): _____

Description: _____

Subject: _____

Notes: _____

Call Number

Your name: _____

People

A Real-Life Hero?

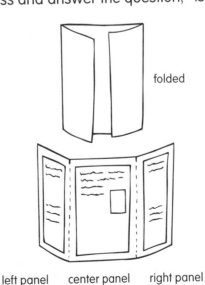

After reading a book about a person, students answer questions about the book and evaluate whether they think the person is a hero.

Materials

- 12" x 18" (30.5 x 45.5 cm) sheet of construction paper
- pages 18 and 19, reproduced for each student
- pencil
- stapler
- marking pens or crayons

Steps to Follow

1. Initiate a class discussion about heroes. Have students brainstorm a list of heroes. Discuss the attributes the heroes have in common. Develop a class definition of a hero.

2. Select a book from the 100s or 300s about a person. Give a brief summary of the book. Share the parts of the book (references to sources, quotes, bibliography, footnotes, etc.) that support the information contained in the book and how the information is presented (graphs, lists of information, reproduction of documents). Then discuss the questions on the response forms (pages 18 and 19). Finally, discuss and answer the question, "Is the person in this book a hero?"

3. Students each read a book of their choice, answer the questions on the response forms about their own books, and tell why the subject of their book is or is not a hero.

4. Students create a folder to hold their response forms. Fold both ends of the construction paper into the center. Staple the report into the folder as shown. Add the book's title, author, and illustrations to the front flaps of the folder.

folded

left panel   center panel   right panel

People

Write a short summary of the book. Add a picture of the person the book is about.

_____

_____

_____

_____

_____

_____

_____

_____

_____

_____

_____

_____

_____

_____

_____

_____

What parts of the book support the information contained in the book?

_____

_____

_____

_____

_____

_____

_____

_____

_____

How is the information presented?

_____

_____

_____

_____

_____

_____

_____

People

My Definition of a Hero

What attributes of heroism are presented in the book?

_____

_____

_____

_____

_____

_____

What attributes of heroism are missing?

_____

_____

_____

_____

_____

_____

Is this book about a hero? Explain your answer.

_____

_____

_____

_____

_____

_____

_____

_____

By _____

People

Survey of Opinions

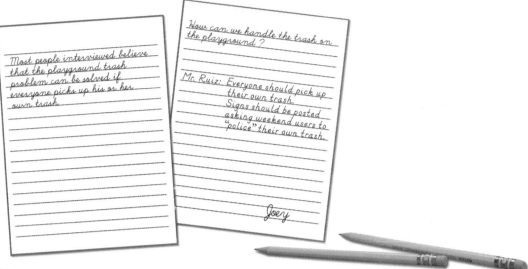

Many books in this category express how people feel about an issue. After selecting a topic, students conduct interviews to determine how others feel about the issue and then write about what has been learned.

Materials

- writing paper
- pencil

Steps to Follow

1. Work together as a class to select a topic relating to some school issue such as homework, cafeteria food, or traffic around the school. State the topic in question form.

   For example:

   What kinds of food do you think should be served in the cafeteria?

   How can traffic be slowed down in front of school at dismissal time?

   Should homework be given over school breaks? Why or why not?

   How can we handle the trash problem on the playground?

   Do state tests improve education?

2. Have students copy the question on a sheet of writing paper. They will use this paper to record responses during their interviews.

3. Each student interviews someone at school about the issue. You may want to assign students to specific people to broaden the scope of the interviews (some students interview other students, some interview school personnel, some interview parents).

4. Compile the results of the interviews. Record the results on the chalkboard or a chart. As a class, generalize what the interviews showed. Discuss how the results support this generalization.

5. Students copy the generalization on the back of their interview sheets. Place this page in the People pockets.

People

Religion and Myths

Bookmark .... **page 22**
Make the bookmark following the instructions on page 2. Review the reading list provided on the bookmark. Ask students to read two nonfiction books about religion or myths.

Catalog Cards .... **page 16**
Students create "catalog cards" as one way to summarize books read in this category. (See page 15 for directions.)

A Myth Book Report .... **pages 23 and 24**
After reading myths, students complete the report form on page 24.

Retell a Myth—
An Accordion Book..................... **pages 25–28**
Students retell their favorite myth as they create an accordion book.

How It Began .... **page 29**
Reread the explanation of how myths originated on page 23. Students then select an event or aspect of nature and write a myth to explain the phenomenon. Provide students with the planning sheet on page 29 and plenty of writing paper.

Religion and Myths

The 200s contain books about beliefs of people past and present. Books on the religions of the world and myths from many cultures are included here.

- *Buddha Stories* by Demi
- *Celebrating Hanukkah* by Diane Hoyt-Goldsmith
- *The Crystal Pool: Myths and Legends of the World* by Geraldine McCaughrean
- *D'Aulaire's Book of Greek Myths* by Ingri and Edgar Parin d'Aulaire
- *The Dead Sea Scrolls* by Ilene Cooper
- *Eyewitness: Bible Lands* by Jonathan N. Tubb
- *Gilgamesh the King* by Ludmila Zeman
- *The Illustrated Book of Myths: Tales and Legends of the World* by Neil Philip
- *In the Beginning* by Virginia Hamilton
- *Odin's Family: Myths of the Vikings* by Neil Philip
- *One World, Many Religions: The Ways We Worship* by Mary Pope Osborne
- *Out of the Ark: Stories from the World's Religions* by Anita Ganeri
- *The Wisdom of the Crows & Other Buddhist Tales* by Sherab Chodzin and Alexandra Kohn

_____

_____

_____

_____

Religion and Myths

©2001 by Evan-Moor Corp. • EMC 2704

A Myth Book Report

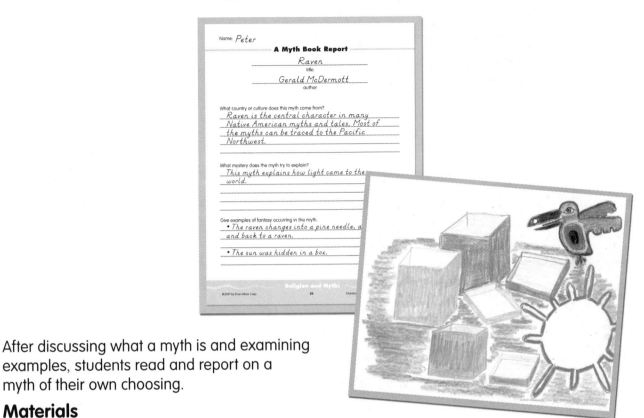

After discussing what a myth is and examining examples, students read and report on a myth of their own choosing.

Materials
- selection of myths from several different countries
- page 24, reproduced for each student
- pencil
- drawing paper

Steps to Follow

1. Discuss what a myth is.

   Ancient peoples tried to explain the mysteries of nature and how things came to be. They lacked the scientific knowledge that we have today, so they created powerful beings who ruled the storms, seasons, stars, the growing of things, love, death, and everyday life. Sometimes they built temples or shrines to these beings and worshiped them as gods and goddesses. As with all stories that are passed on orally, myths grew and changed through the years. Later, some of the myths and legends were written down.

2. Select two or more myths from various cultures (see bookmark on page 22 for some examples). Share summaries of myths with your students. Ask them to figure out what each myth is trying to explain. Have them identify the elements of fantasy in each example.

3. Students select a myth to read. Then they complete the report form on page 24.

4. Students illustrate the myth on a sheet of drawing paper and glue the report to the back of the illustration.

Religion and Myths

A Myth Book Report

_____

title

_____

author

What country or culture does this myth come from?

_____

_____

_____

_____

What mystery does the myth try to explain?

_____

_____

_____

_____

Give examples of fantasy occurring in the myth.

_____

_____

_____

_____

Religion Book Myths

Retell a Myth
An Accordion Book

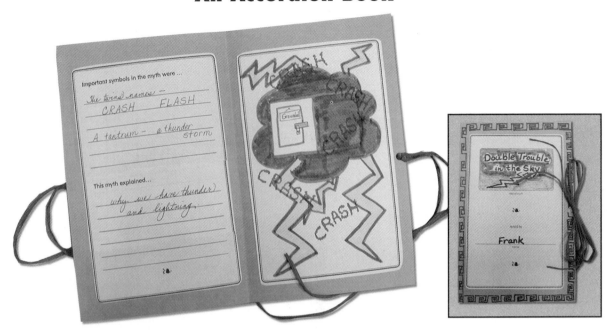

Students retell the events in the myth they read and present the retellings in accordion books.

Materials

- three 9" x 12" (23 x 30.5 cm) pieces of construction paper
- pages 26–28, reproduced for each student
- cellophane tape
- scissors
- glue

- crayons, marking pens, or colored pencils
- two 8" (20 cm) pieces of ribbon or rafia
- writing paper and pencil
- hole punch

Steps to Follow—Book

1. Fold the construction paper in half.
2. Tape the three sheets together.
3. Refold accordion style.
4. Punch one hole in the front and back outer edges.
5. Tie the ribbon in each hole.

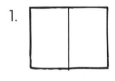

Steps to Follow—Story

1. Read a myth.
2. List the characters and important events that happened in the story.
3. Use this list as a prompt. Retell the myth using the forms on pages 26–28. Draw an illustration on the blank page. Reproduce lined pages as needed. Add borders or illustrations to the story pages.
4. Cut the pages apart and glue them in order on the accordion book.

Religion and Myths

The main characters in this myth are:

The important events in this myth are:

❧

title of myth

❧

retold by

name

❧

In the beginning …

Then …

Important symbols in the myth were ...

This myth explained...

Name: _____

How It Began
Myth Planning Sheet

What natural event is the myth meant to explain? _____

The title of the myth will be: _____

The main characters in this myth are:

_____

_____

_____

These events will occur in the myth:

1. _____

2. _____

3. _____

The conclusion of the myth will be:

_____

_____

_____

Now write your myth on writing paper. Add at least one illustration to your story.

Religion and Myths

Folklore

Make the bookmark following the instructions on page 2. Review the reading list provided on the bookmark. Ask students to read two books of folklore.

Students create "catalog cards" as one way to summarize books read in this category. (See page 15 for directions.)

Students write descriptive paragraphs and create "pull-out" illustrations to present the main character of a piece of folklore they have read.

Students locate and read two versions of the same folktale. Then, using the Venn diagram on page 33, they compare and contrast the two versions. Expand the task by asking them to add illustrations that show an important difference between the two stories.

Using clues from the story, students determine the setting (location and time) of the story they read.

Folklore

Not all books placed in Dewey decimal categories are nonfiction. Folklore (folktales, fairy tales) are shelved in the 300s—the Social Sciences. Read some examples of folklore to see if you can figure out why these fiction stories are placed there.

- *Aesop's Fables* by Jerry Pinkney
- *American Tall Tales* by Mary Pope Osborne
- *Amzat and His Brothers: Three Italian Tales Remembered* by Floriano Vecchi and Paula Fox
- *The Arabian Nights* by Neil Philip
- *Beauty: A Retelling of the Story of Beauty and the Beast* by Robin McKinley
- *The Ch'I-Lin Purse: A Collection of Ancient Chinese Stories* by Linda Fang
- *The Egyptian Cinderella* by Shirley Climo
- *I Know-Not-What, I-Know-Not-Where: A Russian Tale* by Eric Kimmel
- *Little Gold Star: A Spanish American Cinderella Tale* by Robert D. San Souci
- *The New Adventures of Mother Goose* by Bruce Lansky
- *Stories from the Silk Road* by Cherry Gilchrist
- *The Tales of Uncle Remus* by Julius Lester

_____

_____

_____

_____

Folklore

An Expanding Book

Descriptive paragraphs and art highlight the characteristics of the main character from a piece of folklore.

Materials

- 4" x 14" (10 x 35.5 cm) white construction paper
- 5" x 7" (13 x 18 cm) writing paper
- 9" x 12" (23 x 30.5 cm) colored construction paper
- 3" (7.5 cm) square of tagboard
- crayons
- pencil
- scissors
- glue

Steps to Follow

1. Students write a description of the main character of the story read. Remind them that the description should include character traits as well as physical appearance.

2. Sketch and then color the main character of the story on the tagboard square. Cut out the finished illustration.

3. Fold the long white construction paper as shown.

4. Unfold the strip. Students draw an important scene from the story in which the main character takes part. They are to fill in the entire strip of paper. Refold the strip.

5. Glue the right edge of the tag to the folded edge of the scene illustration. Now pull the right-hand side of the paper. The page will expand to show the whole scene.

6. Glue the description of the character to the top of the colored construction paper. Glue the illustration to the bottom of the construction paper.

Folklore

Name: _____

A Tale Told Two Ways

Version 1

_____
title

_____
author

Version 2

_____
title

_____
author

both

Where Is It From?

The illustrations and text contain clues that can help the reader identify the setting of the story.

Materials

- page 35, reproduced for each student
- 9" x 12" (23 x 30.5 cm) colored construction paper
- pencil
- crayons

Steps to Follow

1. Model the activity using a familiar story. List clues to the story's setting taken from the text and illustration. Using this information, ask students to name the setting and time of the story.

   Clues: path going through a forest
   banana trees in the forest
   small wooden houses in a village
   jackal and Bengal tiger in the forest
   the old lady was wearing a sari
   the people ate dinner off of banana leaves

   Setting: a forest and small village in India
   it took place at a hot time of year
   it seemed to be long ago

   Clues: tall snow-covered mountains
   people living in skin tents
   reindeer
   people dressed in clothing made of skin and furs
   traveled by sleds
   storyteller said it happened long ago

   Setting: in the Arctic or Far North
   long ago, but we don't know exactly when

2. After reading a folktale of their own, students complete the form on page 35, describing the location and time of the story they read.

3. Cut apart the forms on page 35. Fold the construction paper in half to make a folder. Glue the title form on the outside of the folder. Glue the description of the setting on the inside of the folder.

Folklore

Look Closely at the Setting

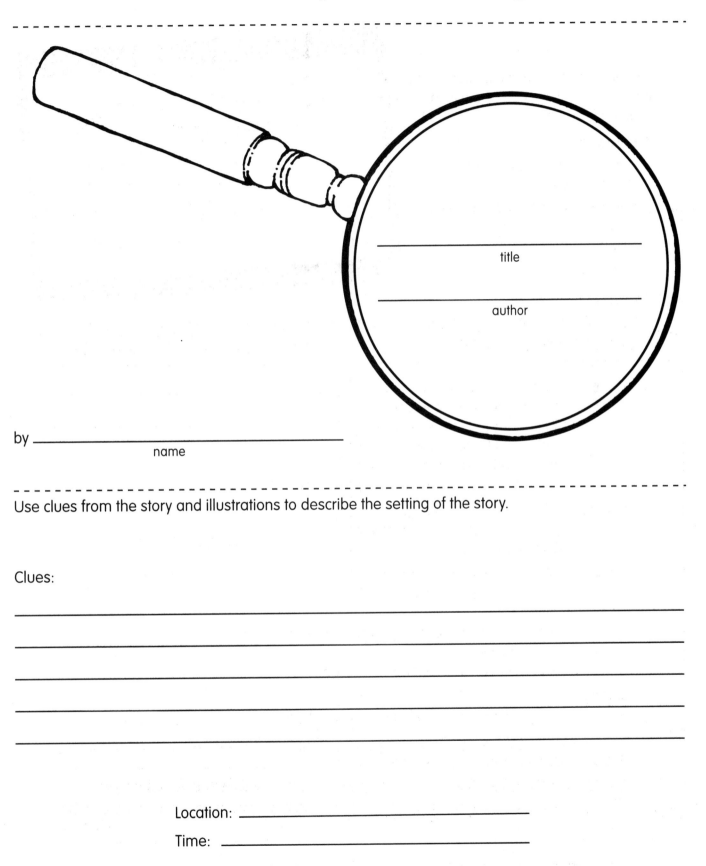

_____
title

_____
author

by _____
name

Use clues from the story and illustrations to describe the setting of the story.

Clues:

_____

_____

_____

_____

_____

Location: _____

Time: _____

Folklore

Language

Bookmark .... **page 37**
Make the bookmark following the instructions on page 2. Review the reading list provided on the bookmark. Ask students to read two books from the language category.

Catalog Cards................................... **page 16**
Students create "catalog cards" as one way to summarize books read in this category. (See page 15 for directions.)

400s Scavenger Hunt .... **page 38**
Individuals or small groups go to the library to explore the types of language materials found in the 400s. Each student is to locate books that meet the requirements on the Scavenger Hunt list.

An ABC Book........................... **pages 39–43**
Challenge students to come up with a new, interesting ABC book to write and illustrate.

It's Part of the Language........... **pages 44–46**
Students select a part of speech (nouns, verbs, etc.) or interesting usage of words (similes, synonyms, figures of speech, etc.) and create colorful booklets.

What's the Message? .... **page 47**
Students read information about nonverbal communication such as sign language, codes, or ancient pictorial languages. Students select one "language" they've read about and complete page 47.

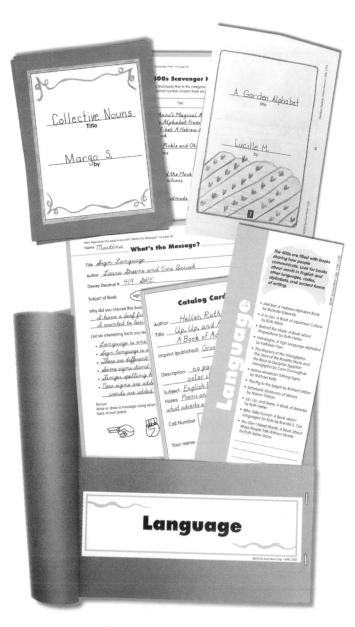

Language

The 400s are filled with books sharing how people communicate. Look for books about words in English and other languages, codes, alphabets, and ancient forms of writing.

- *Alef-bet: A Hebrew Alphabet Book* by Michelle Edwards
- *A to Zen: A Book of Japanese Culture* by Ruth Wells
- *Behind the Mask: A Book about Prepositions* by Ruth Heller
- *Handsigns: A Sign Language Alphabet* by Kathleen Fain
- *The Mystery of the Hieroglyphs: The Story of the Rosetta Stone and the Race to Decipher Egyptian Hieroglyphs* by Carol Donoughue
- *Native American Talking Signs* by Michael Kelly
- *The Pig in the Spigot* by Richard Wilber
- *Scholastic Dictionary of Idioms* by Marvin Terban
- *Up, Up, and Away: A Book of Adverbs* by Ruth Heller
- *Who Talks Funny?: A Book about Languages for Kids* by Brenda S. Cox
- *You Don't Need Words: A Book About Ways People Talk Without Words* by Ruth Belov Gross

_____

_____

_____

_____

Language

Name: _____

400s Scavenger Hunt

Look in the 400s in the library to find books that fit the categories listed below.
Write the title and the Dewey decimal number of each book.

	Title	Dewey Decimal #
Find three alphabet books, each with a different theme.	_____ _____ _____	_____ _____ _____
Find a book about figures of speech.	_____	_____
Find a book about a part of speech.	_____	_____
Find a book that contains nonverbal language.	_____	_____
Find a book written in a foreign language.	_____	_____
Find a book about a language using picture writing such as hieroglyphics.	_____	_____

Language

An ABC Book

After looking at examples of alphabet books with a variety of themes, students create an interesting version of their own.

Materials

- examples of alphabet books with varying themes
- pages 40–43, reproduced for each student (reproduce pages 1/6 and 2/5 back to back; reproduce pages 8/3 and 4/7 back to back)
- scissors
- crayons, marking pens, or colored pencils

Steps to Follow—Words and Illustrations

1. Share a variety of alphabet books with students. Study the ways in which they are alike and how they are unique.

2. Students select a theme. Then they draw an illustration and write a word, phrase, or short sentence to go with each letter of the alphabet.

3. Students write the book title on the cover page and add an interesting illustration.

Steps to Follow—Book Page

1. Fold and cut the two sheets of paper as shown.

Cut the edges of page 40.   Cut the center of page 43.

2. Roll the top and bottom of page 6 and slip it through the hole in the center of the other sheet.

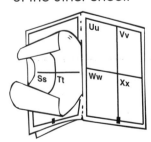 

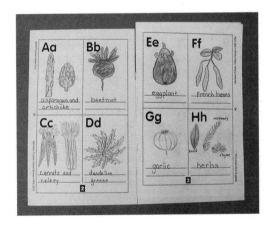

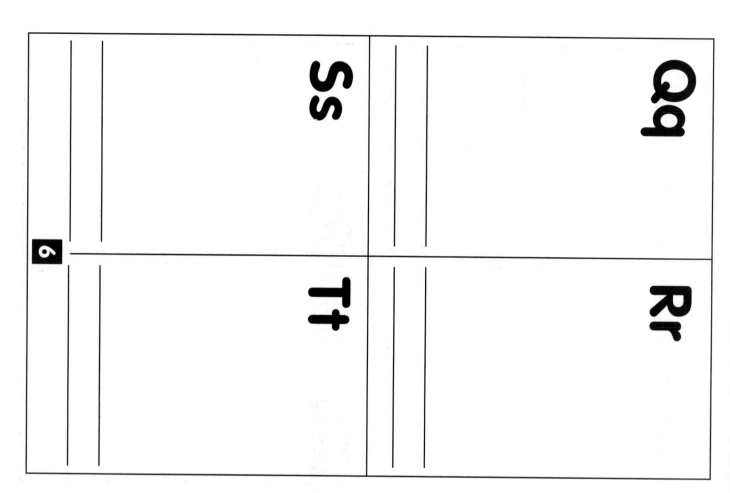

Qq

Rr

Ss

Tt

6

- - - - cut - fold - - - - - - - - - - - - - - - - - - - cut - - - - -

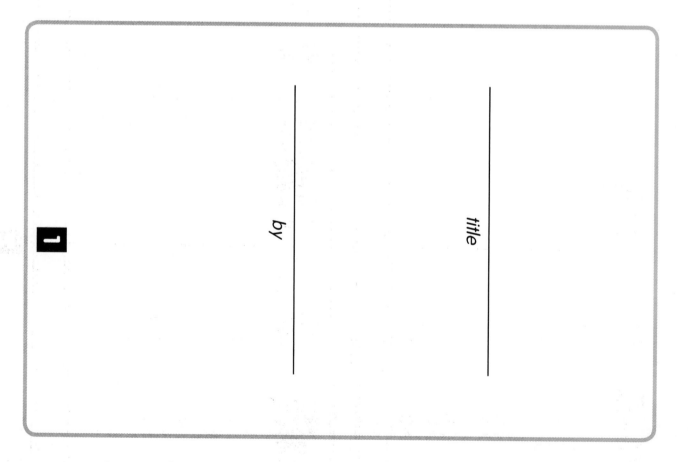

title

by

1

Nn

Mm

Pp

Oo

5

Bb

Aa

Dd

Cc

2

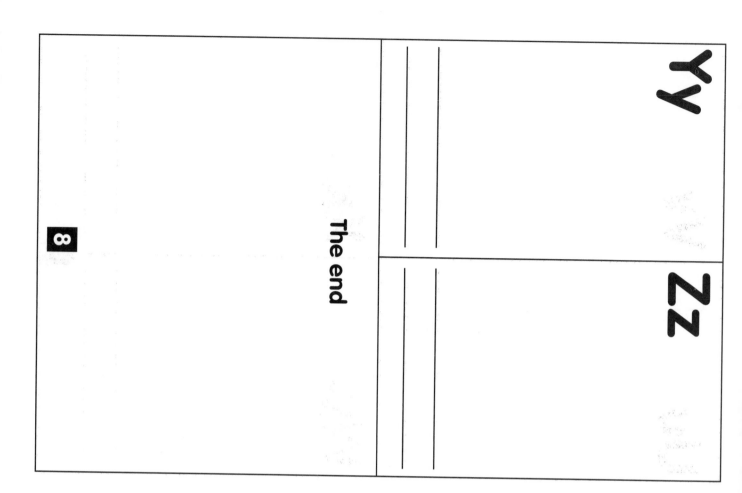

Yy

Zz

The end

8

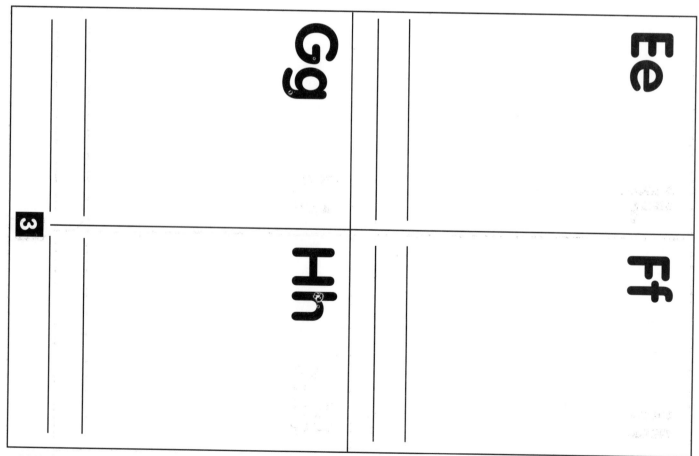

Ee

Ff

Gg

Hh

3

Vv

Uu

Xx

Ww

7

— fold ———— cut ———— fold —

Jj

Ii

Ll

Kk

4

It's Part of the Language

Provide a selection of "word" books from the library (for example, *Behind the Mask: A Book about Prepositions* by Ruth Heller or *A Chocolate Moose for Dinner* by Fred Gwynne). After students have had an opportunity to study the books, they create word books of their own.

Materials

- pages 45 and 46, reproduced for each student
- two 6" x 9" (15 x 23 cm) pieces of construction paper
- scissors
- glue
- pencils
- ruler

Steps to Follow

1. Make a construction paper book following these steps.

a.

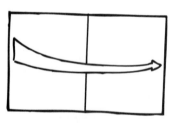

Fold each piece of construction paper in half as shown.

b.

Draw a 3" (7.5 cm) line to the center of the fold line as shown. Cut along this line. Repeat on the other piece of paper.

c.

Slip the pieces of paper together along the cut lines.

2. Select a theme for a "word" book (a part of speech such as nouns, verbs, or adjectives; word usage such as similes, synonyms, or figures of speech). Using the forms on pages 45 and 46, write and illustrate pages.

3. Cut out the completed pages and glue them in order into the paper book.

_____ *Title*

_____ *by*

Definition

_____
_____
_____
_____
_____
_____
_____
_____
_____
_____

Word or Phrase

_____

Word or Phrase

_____

Literature Pockets—Nonfiction • EMC 2704

Word or Phrase

Word or Phrase

Word or Phrase

Word or Phrase

Name: _____

What's the Message?

Title _____

Author _____

Dewey Decimal # _____

Subject of Book: sign language   code   ancient pictorial language

Why did you choose this book to read?

_____

_____

List six interesting facts you learned from this book.

- _____
- _____
- _____
- _____
- _____
- _____

Bonus:
Write or draw a message using what you learned in this book. Write the English translation on the back of your paper.

Language

Nature and Animals

Bookmark .... page 49
Make the bookmark following the instructions on page 2. Review the reading list provided on the bookmark. Ask students to read at least two nonfiction books about animals, habitats, or the weather.

Catalog Cards............................... page 16
Students create "catalog cards" as one way to summarize books read in this category. (See page 15 for directions.)

Habitats .... page 50
After reading about a habitat, students write a report illustrated by pop-up forms.

An Animal Story ....pages 51–53
In this activity, students create a realistic drawing, list facts learned from the story read, and write a realistic fiction story about the animal.

Nature and Animals

Books in the 500s help us understand the world around us. They are books about things found in nature such as wild animals, natural habitats, and the weather.

- *The Biggest Living Thing* by Caroline Arnold
- *Coral Reef: A City That Never Sleeps* by Mary M. Cerullo
- *Elephant Quest* by Ted and Betsy Lewin
- *Gone Forever: An Alphabet of Extinct Animals* by Sandra and William Markle
- *Hawk Highway in the Sky: Watching Raptor Migration* by Caroline Arnold
- *Insect Metamorphosis: From Egg to Adult* by Ron Goor
- *National Audubon Society First Field Guide—Reptiles* by John L. Behler
- *One Day in the Tropical Rain Forest* by Jean Craighead George
- *On the Brink of Extinction: The California Condor* by Caroline Arnold
- *Outside and Inside Birds* by Sandra Markle
- *Safari* by Robert Bateman
- *The Ultimate Dinosaur Book* by David Lambert
- *What Is the Animal Kingdom?* by Bobbie Kalman

_____

_____

_____

_____

Nature and Animals

©2001 by Evan-Moor Corp. • EMC 2704

Habitats

After reading one or more books about a habitat, students create a pop-up report.

Materials

- 9" x 12" (23 x 30.5 cm) construction paper
- two 3" x 6" (7.5 x 15 cm) pieces of construction paper
- two 2" (5 cm) squares of white construction paper
- 4" x 10" (10 x 25.5 cm) writing paper
- glue
- pencil
- crayons or marking pens
- scissors
- stapler

Steps to Follow—Report

1. Select a habitat. Read one or more books about the habitat.

2. Write a report describing the typical features of the habitat and the plants and wildlife that live there.

3. Using the 2" (5 cm) squares of white construction paper, illustrate one animal and one plant appropriate to the habitat.

Steps to Follow—Pop-ups

1. Make two mini-pop-ups with the 3" x 6" (7.5 x 15 cm) pieces of construction paper.

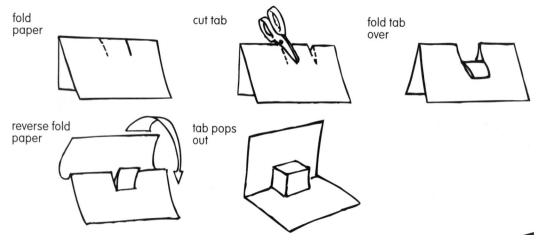

fold paper

cut tab

fold tab over

reverse fold paper

tab pops out

2. Glue the illustrations to the front of the pop-up tab. Close the pop-up and label the front.

3. Staple the report to the left side of the large construction paper. Glue each of the pop-up tabs down the right side of the paper.

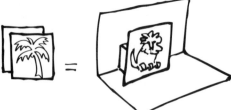

An Animal Story

After reading a nonfiction book about an animal, students list facts they learned, make a naturalistic drawing, and then create a realistic fiction story.

Materials

- pages 52 and 53, reproduced for each student
- writing paper
- pencil
- drawing paper
- drawing pencils or pen and ink
- glue

Steps to Follow

1. Each student reads a nonfiction book about an animal.

2. After studying realistic illustrations of animals in books, students draw the animal using drawing pencils or pen and ink.

3. Using page 52, students list 10 facts they learned about the animal from the book they read. They glue the list of facts to the back of their animal drawings.

4. Provide students with the planning sheet on page 53. Using the facts they collected, students write a realistic fiction story about the animal, including the facts they learned as part of the text.

What a Way to Start a Day!
by Dannette

Early one morning Margo was taking her new puppy for a walk to the park down the street from her house. The puppy bounced around on his big feet, tugging at the leash as if to say "Let me go! You're too slow." The puppy was interested in every sight and every smell in the park. His busy nose kept leading him in a new direction.

As the puppy was exploring his new surroundings, another animal was busy nearby. This little furry creature was at home in the park. In fact, the squirrel had been born in a hole in the park. He quickly ran across a branch hanging on with his sharp claws and using his large, bushy tail for balance. He jumped from branch to branch lower and lower until he reached the ground. The days were getting colder. Soon winter would be here and the squirrel needed to gather and store the food it would need. Fortunately there were acorns scattered all over under the oak tree. The squirrel grabbed the acorns and scampered back up the tree to drop them into his nest. Up and down it ran eager to get as many nuts as possible.

The squirrel was so busy it did not notice the puppy bouncing around the park. But the puppy noticed the squirrel. Suddenly he gave a big tug on his leash and broke free. Away he ran after the squirrel getting between the squirrel and the safety of its tree. The frightened squirrel took off running with the yappy dog following

Name: _____

10 Facts About a _____

1. _____
   _____

2. _____
   _____

3. _____
   _____

4. _____
   _____

5. _____
   _____

6. _____
   _____

7. _____
   _____

8. _____
   _____

9. _____
   _____

10. _____
    _____

Nature and Animals

Name: _____

Realistic Fiction Animal Story
Planning Sheet

1. Who are the **characters** going to be?

   animals:

   people:

2. What is the **setting** going to be?

   location:

   time:

3. What **point of view** will you use?
(animal's point of view or person's point of view)

4. Think about the story **events**. Try to have at least three.
(The final event should be the most exciting.)

5. How will the story end?

Mathematics

Bookmark .... page 55
Make the bookmark following the instructions on page 2. Review the reading list provided on the bookmark. Ask students to read two books about mathematics.

Catalog Cards .... page 16
Students create "catalog cards" as one way to summarize books read in this category. (See page 15 for directions.)

Math Comparisons .... pages 56 and 57
Students use standard and nonstandard measure to make interesting and unusual comparisons.

A Math Dictionary .... pages 58 and 59
Students create their own dictionaries of math terms.

Mathematics

These books help us understand numbers and other aspects of mathematics. You will find these books in the 500s.

- *Anno's Mysterious Multiplying Jar* by Masaichiro and Mitsumasa Anno
- *Can You Count to a Googol?* by Robert E. Wells
- *Do You Wanna Bet?: Your Chance to Find Out about Probability* by Jean Cushman
- *Fantastic Book of Comparisons* by Russell Ash
- *G is for Googol: A Math Alphabet Book* by David Schwartz
- *The History of Counting* by Denise Schmandt-Besserat
- *I Hate Mathematics! Book* by Marilyn Burns
- *Is a Blue Whale the Biggest Thing There Is?* by Robert E. Wells
- *The Librarian Who Measured the Earth* by Kathryn Lasky
- *Math for Smarty Pants* by Marilyn Burns
- *On Beyond a Million: An Amazing Math Journey* by David Schwartz
- *One Grain of Rice: A Mathematical Folktale* by Demi

_____

_____

_____

_____

Mathematics

Math Comparisons

Students make a math comparison involving three forms of measurement—nonstandard, customary, and metric.

Materials

- page 57, reproduced for each student
- 12" x 18" (30.5 x 45.5 cm) construction paper
- stapler
- crayons or marking pens
- glue
- ruler
- 2 paper clips

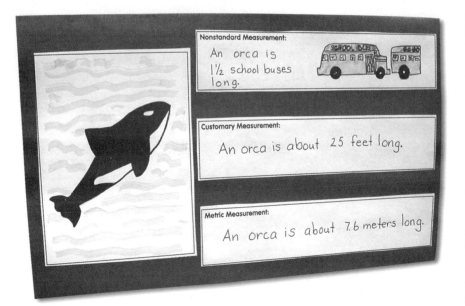

Steps to Follow

1. In preparation for this activity, have students do a library search for books about measurements. For example, *How Tall, How Short, How Faraway* by David Adler, *Incredible Comparisons* by Russell Ash, *Is a Blue Whale the Biggest Thing There Is?* by Robert E. Wells, or *Measuring Penny* by Loreen Leedy. Share these with the class and place them in an accessible location for students to use as they complete their math measurements.

2. Fold the construction paper in half. Measure 2" (5 cm) from the open end. Make a line. Fold both sides.

3. Using page 57, create a math comparison. Draw and label a picture of the item being measured. This can be an object you use every day (pencil, lunch box, football, etc.) or something you have studied about (whale, vehicle, skyscraper, etc.). Include all three types of measurement.

   My pencil is as long as 16 pieces of popped popcorn.

   My pencil is 8 inches long.

   My pencil is 20 centimeters long.

4. Cut the picture and sentences apart and glue them to the construction paper.

5. Using paper clips, place the paper in a stand-up position for display. After displaying, remove the paper clips and place the projects in students' pockets.

Mathematics

Draw the object here.

Nonstandard Measurement:

Customary Measurement:

Metric Measurement:

A Math Dictionary

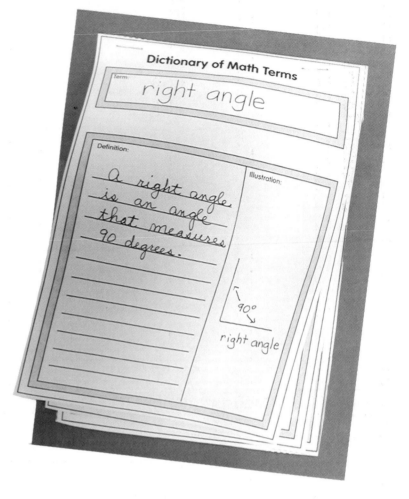

Each student makes a dictionary of math terms. The dictionary must include at least six terms.

Materials

- page 59—three copies reproduced for each student
- 6" x 8" (15 x 20 cm) construction paper
- pencil
- marking pens or colored pencils
- scissors
- stapler

Steps to Follow

1. In preparation for this activity, have students do a library search for books containing explanations of math terms. For example, *Angles* by Marion Smoothey, *Everything You Need to Know About Math Homework* by Anne Zeman, or *G is for Googol: A Math Alphabet Book* by David Schwartz. Share these with the class and place them in an accessible location for students to use as they develop their list of math terms and definitions.

2. Select six math terms. These may be general terms (*multiplication, zero, fraction, divisor*) or about a specific math theme or concept (*triangle, oval, hexagon, volume, area, perimeter*).

3. Complete a form for each math term. Write the definition and add an illustration for each term.

4. Put the words in alphabetical order and staple them to the construction paper.

Mathematics

Dictionary of Math Terms

Term:

Illustration:

Definition:

Dictionary of Math Terms

Term:

Illustration:

Definition:

Literature Pockets—Nonfiction • EMC 2704

Science and Technology

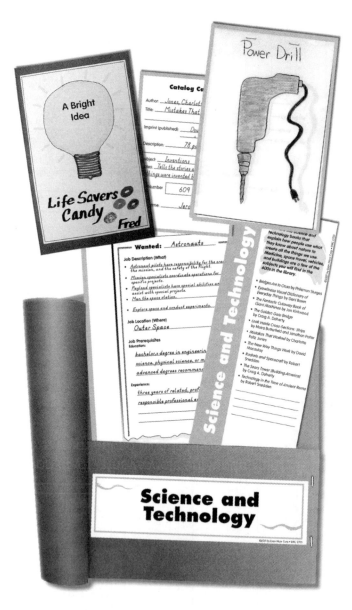

Bookmark .... page 61
Make the bookmark following the instructions on page 2. Review the reading list provided on the bookmark. Ask students to read two nonfiction books about science or technology.

Catalog Cards................................. page 16
Students create "catalog cards" as one way to summarize books read in this category. (See page 15 for directions.)

A Bright Idea .... pages 62–65
Students read about an invention and then answer the questions on pages 63–65 to create a "Bright Idea" book.

Wanted—A Job Description ... pages 66 and 67
Students write a job description for a scientific or technological occupation.

What's Inside? .... page 68
Using library resources, students take a close look at the insides of machinery. Then they draw and label the working parts of one kind of machine.

Science and Technology

Here are the science and technology books that explain how people use what they know about nature to create all the things we use. Medicine, space travel, vehicles, and buildings are a few of the subjects you will find in the 600s in the library.

- *Bridges Are to Cross* by Philemon Sturges
- *Eyewitness Visual Dictionary of Everyday Things* by Deni Bown
- *The Fantastic Cutaway Book of Giant Machines* by Jon Kirkwood
- *The Golden Gate Bridge* by Craig A. Doherty
- *Look Inside Cross-Sections: Ships* by Moira Butterfield and Jonathan Potter
- *Mistakes That Worked* by Charlotte Foltz Jones
- *The New Way Things Work* by David Macaulay
- *Rockets and Spacecraft* by Robert Snedden
- *The Sears Tower (Building America)* by Craig A. Doherty
- *Technology in the Time of Ancient Rome* by Robert Snedden

_____

_____

_____

_____

Science and Technology

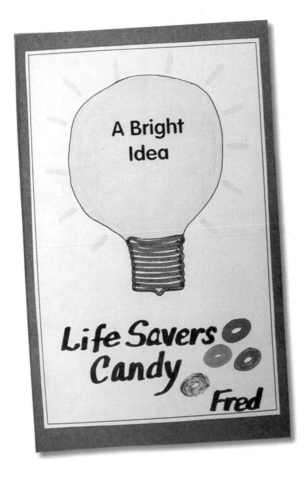

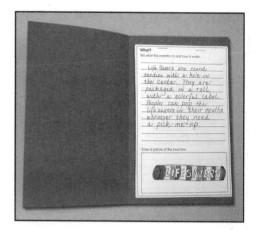

Students read about inventions and then select one to explore more thoroughly. Using the forms provided, students compile a simple invention report.

Materials

- pages 63–65, reproduced for each student
- 8" x 10" (20 x 25.5 cm) construction paper
- scissors
- pencil
- glue
- stapler
- crayons or marking pens

Steps to Follow

1. After reading about an invention, students complete their report using pages 63–65. Cut the completed report pages apart.

2. Fold the construction paper in half to use as a cover. Glue the Bright Idea form to the front cover.

3. Staple the report pages inside the cover.

Science and Technology

What?

Tell what the invention is and how it works.

_____
_____
_____
_____
_____
_____
_____
_____
_____
_____
_____

Draw a picture of the invention.

A Bright Idea

Who?
Tell who invented it.

When?
Tell when it was invented.

I have a bright idea!

Describe your idea.

Why?

Tell why the invention is important.

Wanted
A Job Description

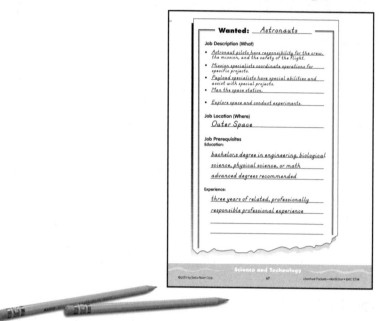

What are the qualifications for a job as a chemist, a geologist, or an astronomer? There are hundreds of scientific and technological jobs. Students learn more about what these people do and what they must know.

Materials

- page 67—make an overhead transparency and reproduce for each student
- pencil
- writing paper

Steps to Follow

1. Study several books about different areas of science and types of scientists. Select one area of science and a type of scientist working in that area. Use that scientist to model the activity. Fill in the sections of the overhead transparency as the class answers these questions:

   What does the scientist do?

   What kind of education and experience is necessary?

   What characteristics and talents will help with this job?

2. Divide students into small groups. Ask each group to select a type of scientist to research. They take notes on writing paper and use them as they complete the form on page 67. They are to include a description of the job, where the job will be located, and the education and experience required.

3. Each group selects one member to share what they learned with the class.

Science and Technology

Wanted: _____

Job Description (What)

- _____

- _____

- _____

- _____

- _____

Job Location (Where)

_____

Job Prerequisites
Education:

_____

_____

_____

Experience:

_____

_____

_____

_____

Science and Technology

What's Inside?

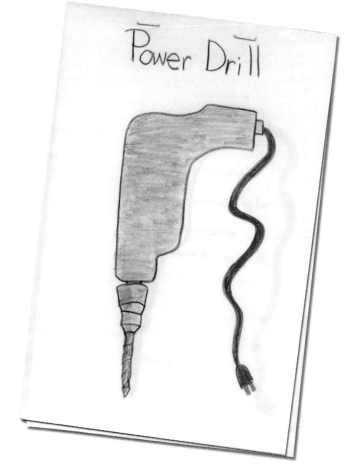

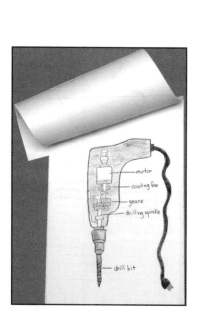

Using library resources, students take a close look at the insides of machinery.

Materials

- two 6" x 9" (15 x 23 cm) pieces of white drawing paper
- writing paper cut to 6" x 9" (15 x 23 cm)
- crayons, colored pencils, or marking pens
- pencil

Steps to Follow

1. In preparation for this activity, students do a search of the 600s in the library to locate books containing cross-sections of machinery. Present these to the class, pointing out appropriate illustrations. Place the books in an accessible location for students to use as they complete the activity.

2. Students select one type of machine to illustrate. They draw the outside of the machine on one piece of drawing paper and the inside on the other. They then label parts where possible.

3. Students write a paragraph describing how the machine works and staple the pages together.

Science and Technology

Arts, Sports, and Recreation

Bookmark .... page 70
Make the bookmark following the instructions on page 2. Review the reading list provided on the bookmark. Ask students to read two nonfiction books about art, sports, or some form of recreation.

Catalog Cards .... page 16
Students create "catalog cards" as one way to summarize books read in this category. (See page 15 for directions.)

**How to Play the Game—
A Shape Book** .... pages 71 and 72
Love sports? What's your favorite? Students develop a guide to help others learn more about their favorite sports and how to play them.

A Work of Art .... pages 73 and 74
After reading about an art medium, artist, or art style, students use what they learned to create a work of art. If the project is large or three-dimensional, take a photograph of it to place in the literature pocket.

Recreation .... page 75
Brainstorm and list all the different kinds of recreation people experience. Then students list their favorite kinds of recreation and write a definition of *recreation*.

Arts, Sports, and Recreation

Here's a chance to read about the wonderful ways to fill one's leisure time. Fine arts, sports, and recreational activities are all contained in the 700s.

©2001 by Evan-Moor Corp. • EMC 2704

- *Angela Weaves a Dream: The Story of a Young Maya Artist* by Michèle Solá
- *Alvin Ailey* by Andrea Davis Pinkney
- *Arthur Ashe* by Caroline Evensen Lazo
- *A Young Painter—The Life and Paintings of Wang Yani* by Zheng Zhensun
- *Batboy: An Inside Look at Spring Training* by Joan Anderson
- *I See Rhythm* by Toyomi Igus
- *Painters of the Caves* by Patricia Lauber
- *Special Effects in Film and Television* by Jake Hamilton
- *Techno Lab: How Science Is Changing Entertainment* by Carol D. Anderson
- *The Top of the World: Climbing Mount Everest* by Steve Jenkins
- *William Shakespeare & the Globe* by Aliki
- *Wilma Unlimited* by Kathleen Krull
- *Young Tennis Player* by Arantxa Sanches Vicario

_____

_____

_____

_____

©2001 by Evan-Moor Corp. • EMC 2704

Arts, Sports, and Recreation

How to Play the Game
A Shape Book

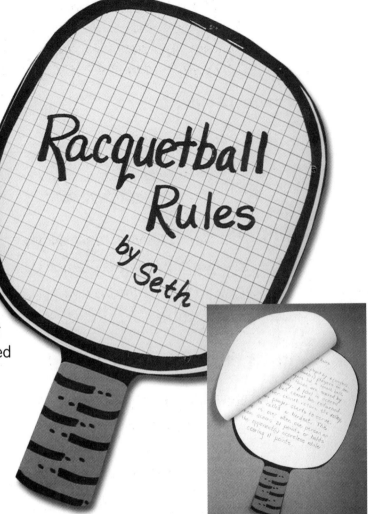

After reading books about different sports, students create a shape book containing the rules for their favorite sport.

Materials

- page 72, reproduced for each student
- 9" x 12" (23 x 30.5 cm) pieces of colored construction paper
- writing paper
- 9" x 12" (23 x 30.5 cm) drawing paper
- construction paper scraps
- crayons or colored marking pens
- scissors
- glue

Steps to Follow—Book

1. Students select some piece of equipment appropriate to the sport they are writing about and use it as the shape for their book. They design the cover and cut it out of construction paper. Construction paper scraps may be used to add details.

2. They write the name of the sport on the cover with crayons or marking pens.

3. Students trace around the book shape on white drawing paper and writing paper. Then they cut out the paper in the same shape as the cover.

Steps to Follow—Rules

1. Students plan their rule books using page 72. Encourage students to write down key words and phrases.

2. Using the information on the checklist, they write their books. Then they add illustrations and a diagram of the playing field on white drawing paper.

3. Staple the pages in order inside the cover.

Arts, Sports, and Recreation

How to Play the Game
Planning Checklist

_____
name of game

☐ Number of players: _____

☐ Positions (if special to the game): _____

☐ Equipment needed: _____

☐ Time periods (if any): _____

☐ Where is the game played? _____

☐ Rules for the game: _____

_____

_____

_____

_____

_____

☐ Penalties (if any): _____

_____

☐ How the game is won: _____

_____

☐ Special vocabulary: _____

_____

_____

Arts, Sports, and Recreation

A Work of Art

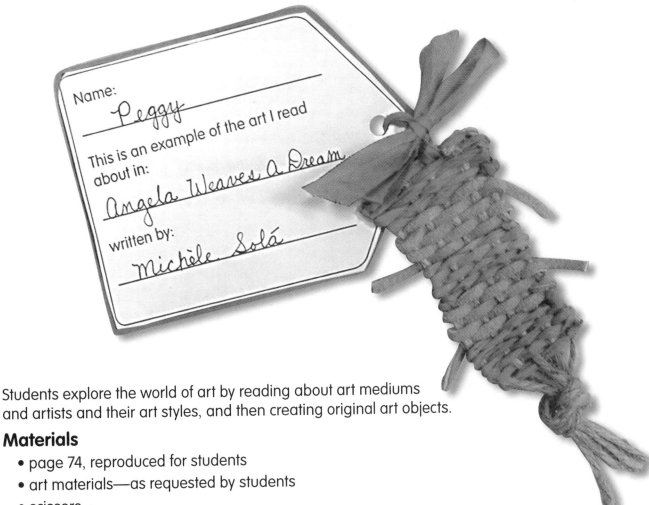

Name: Peggy

This is an example of the art I read about in:

Angela Weaves A Dream

written by:

Michèle Solá

Students explore the world of art by reading about art mediums and artists and their art styles, and then creating original art objects.

Materials
- page 74, reproduced for students
- art materials—as requested by students
- scissors
- glue
- hole punch
- 12" (30.5 cm) string or narrow ribbon

Steps to Follow
1. Read about various art forms, mediums, and artists. Then have students select one technique, medium, or style to explore further by completing an art project.

2. Students list and collect materials needed for their particular project.

3. Students complete their projects. Then students fill in an identification label (see page 74). Punch a hole in the corner of the tag and tie it to the completed project.

4. Display the art projects for everyone to enjoy. When the projects are removed from the display, place them in students' pockets. If the project won't fit in the pocket, photograph it and put the photo in the pocket.

Name: _____

This is an example of the art I read about in: _____

written by: _____

Name: _____

This is an example of the art I read about in: _____

written by: _____

Name: _____

This is an example of the art I read about in: _____

written by: _____

Name: _____

This is an example of the art I read about in: _____

written by: _____

Arts, Sports, and Recreation

Name:

Recreation

Write a definition of *recreation*.

_____

_____

List four things you do for recreation.

1. _____

2. _____

3. _____

4. _____

Illustrate your favorite kind of recreation.

     Literature Pockets—Nonfiction • EMC 2704

Poetry and Plays

Bookmark .... **page 77**
Make the bookmark following the instructions on page 2. Review the reading list provided on the bookmark. Ask students to read at least one play and one book of poetry.

Catalog Cards .... **page 16**
Students create "catalog cards" as one way to summarize books read in this category. (See page 15 for directions.)

Autobiographical Poem .... **pages 78 and 79**
Students write autobiographical poems using the planning form on page 79.

The Play's the Thing .... **pages 80–82**
This activity asks students to determine the differences and similarities between a story and a play.

My Favorite Poem .... **page 83**
After reading several books of poetry, students select a short poem they liked and copy it on the form on page 83. Then they turn the paper over and write an explanation of why they selected that poem.

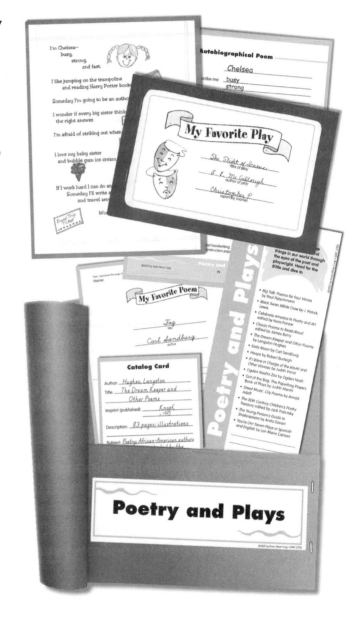

Poetry and Plays

Here is a chance to see the people, places, and things in our world through the eyes of the poet and playwright. Head for the 800s and dive in.

- *Big Talk: Poems for Four Voices* by Paul Fleischmann
- *Black Swan White Crow* by J. Patrick Lewis
- *Celebrate America In Poetry and Art* edited by Nora Panzer
- *Classic Poems to Read Aloud* edited by James Berry
- *The Dream Keeper and Other Poems* by Langston Hughes
- *Early Moon* by Carl Sandburg
- *Hoops* by Robert Burleigh
- *If I Were in Charge of the World and Other Worries* by Judith Viorst
- *Ogden Nash's Zoo* by Ogden Nash
- *Out of the Bag: The Paperbag Players Book of Plays* by Judith Martin
- *Street Music: City Poems* by Arnold Adoff
- *The 20th Century Children's Poetry Treasury* edited by Jack Prelutsky
- *The Young Person's Guide to Shakespeare* by Anita Ganeri
- *You're On! Seven Plays in Spanish and English* by Lori Marie Carlson

_____

_____

_____

_____

Poetry and Plays

©2001 by Evan-Moor Corp. • EMC 2704

Autobiographical Poem

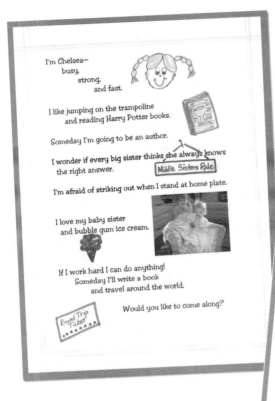

Students follow a pattern to create poems about themselves.

Materials

- page 79, reproduced for each student
- writing paper
- pencil
- 9" x 12" (23 x 30.5 cm) colored construction paper
- glue

Steps to Follow

1. Review the rough draft form on page 79 to clarify what is being asked in each step. Ask students to provide examples of what might be included at each step. Remind students to use words and phrases rather than complete sentences.

2. Students complete their rough drafts, working with the words until they are satisfied with what they have written. They then copy their poems on writing paper.

3. Glue the finished poem to construction paper. Add a photograph or a drawing to complete the page.

Autobiographical Poem

My name: _____

These three adjectives describe me: _____

_____

_____

This is what I like to do right now. _____

_____

This is what I dream of becoming. _____

This is something I wonder about. _____

_____

This is something I fear. _____

_____

This is what I believe. _____

_____

These are two things I love. _____

_____

These are two things I plan to do. _____

_____

Add a closing line. _____

Now copy your completed poem in your best handwriting. Add an illustration, a photograph, or a border. Glue the poem to a sheet of construction paper in your favorite color.

 Literature Pockets—Nonfiction • EMC 2704

The Play's the Thing

What are the components of a play? How is a play different from a story? Students read a play to find the answers to these questions.

Materials
- pages 81 and 82, reproduced for each student
- two 5" x 7" (13 x 18 cm) pieces of colored construction paper
- glue
- scissors
- pencil
- stapler
- crayons or marking pens

Steps to Follow
1. After reading several plays, discuss the parts of a play (plot presented in dialog, stage directions, directions given for sets and costumes, divided into scenes within acts). List these on the chalkboard.

2. Review the characteristics of a story (written in narrative style, story usually told through one character's point of view, setting described in text, illustrations sometimes used to show setting or events, longer stories divided into chapters, etc.).

3. Each student reads a play. Using page 81 and 82, students summarize and evaluate the play they read.

4. They then make a comparison to show the ways in which plays and stories are alike and different.

5. Cut apart the forms. Glue the title page on one sheet of construction paper. Place the remaining parts of the report between the construction paper sheets and staple on the left side.

Poetry and Plays

My Favorite Play

_____
title of play

_____
author of play

_____
report by (name)

Play Summary

_____

_____

_____

_____

_____

_____

_____

_____

_____

_____

Play Evaluation

_____

_____

_____

_____

_____

_____

_____

_____

_____

Comparison of a Play and Story

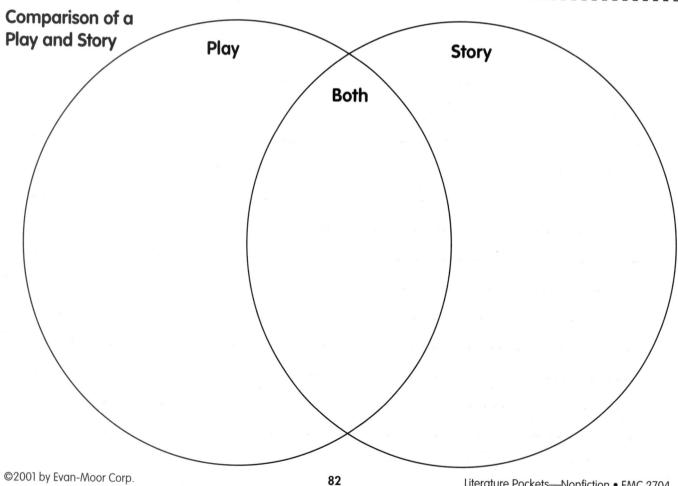

Play   Story

Both

Note: Reproduce this page for students to use with "My Favorite Poem" on page 76.

Name: _____

_____
title

_____
author

_____
_____
_____
_____
_____
_____
_____
_____
_____
_____
_____
_____

History and Travel

Bookmark .... **page 85**
Make the bookmark following the instructions on page 2. Review the reading list provided on the bookmark. Ask students to read a nonfiction travel book and a history book.

Catalog Cards .... **page 16**
Students create "catalog cards" as one way to summarize books read in this category. (See page 15 for directions.)

Historical Catalog .... **pages 86 and 87**
Students create a little catalog of items from one historical period they read about.

Ticket to _____ .... **pages 88 and 89**
Students write journal entries for a "trip" to a specific place. They complete the "ticket" on page 89 to identify the book they read and the location of the journey.

What an Event! .... **page 90**
After reading a history book, students complete the note taker on page 90 to report on one important event they learned about.

History and Travel

History books provide a record of events that occurred and the people who participated in the events. The 900s also contain geography and travel books to help us learn about other places and people living in our world.

- *Around the World in a Hundred Years: from Henry the Navigator to Magellan* by Jean Fritz
- *At Home with the Presidents* by Juddi Morris
- *52 Days by Camel: My Sahara Adventure* by Lawrence Raskin
- *The Gettysburg Address* by Abraham Lincoln and Michael McCurdy
- *On Board the Titanic* by Shelley Tanaka
- *Scholastic Encyclopedia of the North American Indian* by James Ciment
- *The Silk Route: 7,000 Miles of History* by John S. Major
- *Tell Them We Remember: The Story of the Holocaust* by Susan D. Bachrach
- *Tibet: Through the Red Box* by Peter Sis

_____

_____

_____

_____

History and Travel

©2001 by Evan-Moor Corp. • EMC 2704

Historical Catalog

Students make this little "poof" book that contains a catalog of items from some historical period.

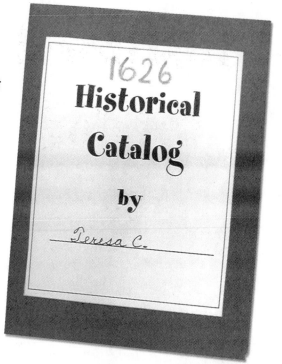

Materials

- page 87—two copies reproduced for each student
- 12" x 18" (30.5 x 45.5 cm) construction paper
- scissors
- glue
- pencil
- crayons or marking pens

Steps to Follow—Poof Book

1. Fold the large piece of construction paper as shown.

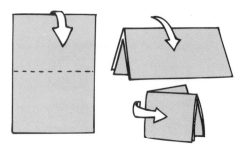

2. Open the paper again and cut on the fold as shown, stopping at the horizontal fold.

3. Fold in half. Push in the ends. "Poof," you have a minibook.

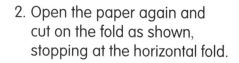
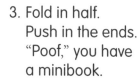
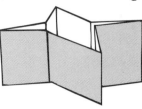

Steps to Follow—Catalog Pages

1. Read several historical books. Then select a period of interest and list items to go in the catalog (clothing, tools, everyday items used at home, vehicles, etc.).

2. Complete the entries including the name of the item, an illustration, and a description of how it was used.

3. Cut apart the writing forms. Glue one on each page. Design a front cover.

Historical Catalog

by

_____

_____ item

Picture

Description

_____

_____ item

Picture

Description

_____ item

Picture

Description

Ticket To _____

After reading a travel book, students create a ticket and journal about an imaginary trip they could make to that location.

Materials
- page 89, reproduced for each student
- 3" x 4" (7.5 x 10 cm) construction paper
- 12" (30.5 cm) string or ribbon
- hole punch
- glue
- scissors

Steps to Follow
1. Go over the forms on page 89. Discuss the types of information needed to complete the ticket, and what might be included in a journal entry (mode of travel used on the journey, where they traveled, highlights of the trip, etc.).

2. Students fill in the information on the ticket. Then they cut the ticket form apart and glue one part of the ticket to each side of the construction paper.

3. Next, complete three or more entries for a journal about the trip. Staple the pages together.

4. Punch a hole in the corner of the ticket and the corner of the journal pages. Tie them together with a piece of string or ribbon.

History and Travel

front:

back:

Ticket to:

_____
location of journey

via _____
name of book read

Evaluation Checklist

☐ I can't wait to go again.

☐ It was okay.

☐ I should have stayed at home.

Journal Entry #1

Journal Entry #2

Journal Entry #3

Name:

What an Event!

Name of event:

When it occurred:

What happened?

_____

_____

_____

_____

_____

_____

_____

Where did it occur?

_____

_____

_____

_____

_____

_____

_____

Who does it involve?

_____

_____

_____

_____

_____

_____

Significance in history?

_____

_____

_____

_____

_____

_____

History and Travel

Biography

Bookmark .... **page 92**
Make the bookmark following the instructions on page 2. Review the reading list provided on the bookmark. Ask students to read biographies of two different people.

Catalog Cards .... **page 16**
Students create "catalog cards" as one way to summarize books read in this category. (See page 15 for directions.)

An Oral Report .... **pages 93–95**
After reading one or more biographies about a person, students write a report that includes an oral presentation and some graphic elements.

Write a Biography .... **page 96**
Students interview and write biographies about interesting people they know.

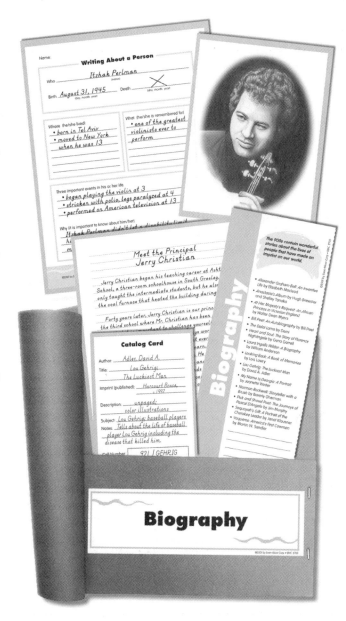

Biography

The 900s contain wonderful stories about the lives of people that have made an imprint on our world.

- *Alexander Graham Bell: An Inventive Life* by Elizabeth Macleod
- *Anastasia's Album* by Hugh Brewster and Shelley Tanaka
- *At Her Majesty's Request: An African Princess in Victorian England* by Walter Dean Myers
- *Bill Peet: An Autobiography* by Bill Peet
- *The Dalai Lama* by Demi
- *Heart and Soul: The Story of Florence Nightingale* by Gena Gorrell
- *Laura Ingalls Wilder: A Biography* by William Anderson
- *Looking Back: A Book of Memories* by Lois Lowry
- *Lou Gehrig: The Luckiest Man* by David A. Adler
- *My Name Is Georgia: A Portrait* by Jeanette Winter
- *Norman Rockwell: Storyteller with a Brush* by Beverly Gherman
- *Pick and Shovel Poet: The Journeys of Pascal D'Angelo* by Jim Murphy
- *Sequoyah's Gift: A Portrait of the Cherokee Leader* by Janet Klausner
- *Vaqueros: America's First Cowmen* by Martin W. Sandler

_____

_____

_____

_____

Biography

An Oral Report

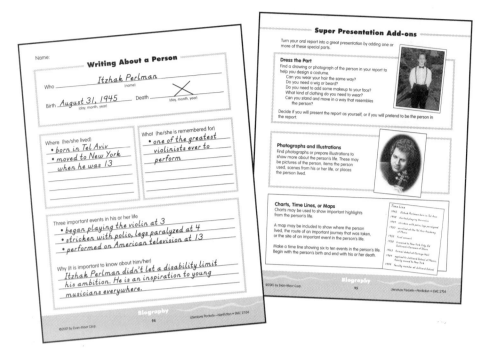

After reading biographies about interesting people, students practice writing and speaking skills by presenting oral reports.

Materials

- pages 94 and 95, reproduced for each student
- access to a variety of types of paper (for making charts, graphs, and maps)
- crayons, marking pens, colored pencils
- writing paper
- pencil
- costume materials (students bring from home; provide assistance where necessary)

Steps to Follow

1. Discuss the parts to be included in the oral report:

   oral presentation about the person
   one or more graphic components (map, chart, time line, photos, drawings)
   dress as the person

2. After reading a biography, students use the note taker on page 94 to record pertinent information. They then decide on one or more ways to add interest and information to the oral presentation (see page 95).

3. Students prepare a 3- to 5-minute oral report using the information on the note taker. They then prepare graphic components and collect materials for the costume.

4. Provide time each day for a few students to present their oral reports. Take a photograph of each student in costume. This will be placed in the student's Biography pocket along with the note taker and any graphics created for the presentation.

Biography

Name: _____

Writing About a Person

Who _____
                    (name)

Birth _____   Death _____
            (day, month, year)   (day, month, year)

Where (he/she lived)

_____

_____

_____

_____

_____

_____

What (he/she is remembered for)

_____

_____

_____

_____

_____

_____

Three important events in his or her life

_____

_____

_____

Why (it is important to know about him/her)

_____

_____

_____

Biography

Super Presentation Add-ons

Turn your oral report into a great presentation by adding one or more of these special parts.

Dress the Part

Find a drawing or photograph of the person in your report to help you design a costume.

Can you wear your hair the same way?
Do you need a wig or beard?
Do you need to add some makeup to your face?
What kind of clothing do you need to wear?
Can you stand and move in a way that resembles the person?

Decide if you will present the report as yourself, or if you will pretend to be the person in the report.

Photographs and Illustrations

Find photographs or prepare illustrations to show more about the person's life. These may be pictures of the person, items the person used, scenes from his or her life, or places the person lived.

Charts, Time Lines, or Maps

Charts may be used to show important highlights from the person's life.

A map may be included to show where the person lived, the route of an important journey that was taken, or the site of an important event in the person's life.

Make a time line showing six to ten events in the person's life. Begin with the person's birth and end with his or her death.

Time Line

1945 Itzhak Perlman born in Tel Aviv
1948 started playing the violin
1949 stricken with polio, legs paralyzed
1950 enrolled at the Tel Aviv Academy of Music
1955 first concert
1958 traveled to New York City, Ed Sullivan's Caravan of Stars
1963 formal debut at Carnige Hall
1964 applied to Julliard School of Music, family moved to New York
1999 faculty member at Julliard School

Biography

Note: Reproduce this page for students to use with "Write a Biography" on page 91.

Write a Biography

After reading biographies, students write one about an interesting person they know.

Materials

- writing paper
- pencil
- chart paper
- black marking pen
- crayons or colored pencils

Steps to Follow

1. Brainstorm and list questions that might be asked when interviewing a person. Write the following on a sheet of chart paper:

   When and where were you born?

   Where did you grow up? Describe your childhood.

   Tell about your schooling.

   What work do you do? How did you learn to do this?

   What special interests do you enjoy?

   Describe your talents.

   What are your future dreams and ambitions?

   Who do you admire most? Why?

   What have you done in your life that you are proudest of?

2. Invite a member of the staff, a parent, or a student to help as you model how to interview a person. Select a student to record notes on the chalkboard as the interview takes place.

   At this point, you may choose to have everyone write a biography of the person interviewed, using the information on the chalkboard.

   Or, have each student interview someone they know and write a biography of that person. In this case, reproduce copies of the questions developed in step one for students to use as they conduct their interviews.

3. After writing the biography, students draw a picture of the person and one or more important events from his or her life to include with the report.

4. Students include a photograph with their completed report.

Biography